7

a Day to Mastering the Craft of Writing

**A Step-by-Step Guide to Becoming
a Better Fiction Writer**

By Rob Bignell

Atiswinic Press · Ojai, Calif.

7 MINUTES A DAY TO MASTERING
THE CRAFT OF WRITING
A Step-by-Step Guide to Becoming
a Better Fiction Writer

Copyright Rob Bignell, 2013

Atiswinic Press
Ojai, Calif. 93023
inventingrealityediting.wordpress.com/home

ISBN 978-0-9896723-3-7
LCCN 2013919887

Cover design by Douglas F. Fullmer
Back cover photo by Bryan Bignell

Manufactured in the United States of America
First printing November 2013

DEDICATION
For Kieran

Table of Contents

Introduction: What is "The Craft of Writing"?

"Writing is easy. All you do is cross out all the wrong words." – Mark Twain

You've written an action-packed plot full of great twists. It's got fascinating characters who grow and develop. You've maintained a consistent point of view, provided incredible descriptions of the setting, and even offered a profound message.

Yet, every time you read the story, it feels flat. Vanilla. Dare I even say...boring?

As a long-time novel and short story editor, I've read hundreds of manuscripts in which this was the case. Clearly the writer grasped some basics of storytelling. But like a comic who understands what makes a joke funny yet can't get his audience to laugh, something in the story was missing.

After analyzing those manuscripts, I realized that many shared the same flaws...lots of passive voice...lots of exposition...lots of fat writing. Unfortunately, these authors had not yet mastered the *craft of writing*. Their delivery fell short.

In comedy, delivery is just as important as the words of the joke. Arguably, it's a good portion of what makes the joke funny. Likewise with storytelling, craft is as important as the plot or characters.

Techniques such as varying sentence lengths, using active rather than passive voice, and avoiding clichés all make one's writing stronger. Recognizing these methods is important because style can be the difference between readers buying more of your books or giving you a bad review at Amazon.com.

The book you now hold in your hands, "7 Minutes a Day to Mastering the Craft of Writing," will help elevate you from crude apprentice to respected craftsman – and it'll only require a few minutes a day.

This book offers a step-by-step guide to improving your fiction writing, whether you're penning a short story, novella or novel. Simply set aside seven minutes a day – between classes, in the morning before your family gets up, or during lunch at work. In that time, take a minute or two to read one "step" of this book. Then for another five minutes edit and write as instructed in the "You Do It" section that follows each step.

Each writing you complete for a "You Do It" section builds upon the previous one, allowing you to quickly rewrite your story or a novel chapter.

To achieve this, you'll need a couple of tools. First, you must have a story or a novel chapter that you've already written. The presumption is that you've picked up this book because you're dissatisfied with what you're writing and recognize that craftsmanship is the problem. Secondly, you'll need a timer, such as one on your watch, cell phone or microwave, so that you spend only seven minutes a day on your writing. Of course, you don't have to limit yourself to seven minutes. By all means, if you can dedicate 10 minutes, 30 minutes, or an hour a day, do so. The more you write, the better.

But you'll need a minimum of seven minutes a day to complete each writing exercise. Should you need more time than the seven minutes, go back the following day and complete it before moving on to the next step.

After a couple of weeks of reading "7 Minutes a Day to Mastering the Craft of Writing" and revising as the "You Do It" sections instruct, you'll begin to see a better story emerge. It will be an amazing experience for you. You'll soon start to realize the talent you always knew you had...at the very least, you'll discover that simply taking a few minutes a day to practice your craft will lead to some impressive results.

So what are you waiting for? Let's get started becoming a better writer now!

Voice

Ever notice how you can identify some authors by the way they write? That's because they have a distinct voice. Each writer sounds unique because each of has our own world view. Someone who is cynical likely is to write in a cynical style. He accomplishes this by creating rhythm and diction, by shaping sentences. These stylistic techniques create a certain pattern or texture in one's writing. In the steps ahead, we'll look at how you as a writer establish "voice" in your fiction and then discuss some ways you can cultivate it.

Step 1. Develop a Sense of Voice

All authors who master their craft write in a certain style or "voice." Every good author makes the story his own by giving it a distinct personality.

Consider this snippet from a short story:

He found the night sky beautiful and mysterious. The heavens grew inkier the higher one looked, as if space suddenly were denser there. A streak of brilliant white light moving west, the Saoirse Comet, shined amid the stars. The fuzzy edges of the silhouetted corn leaves wavered above him, breaking his view of the firmament, and he resisted a tear.

Now compare it to this sample from another piece:

Endless sky. Trail heading nowhere. Small rocks everywhere. Before you, under your foot, beside you. Hills browned with what passed for grass. Keep moving. No reason to stop. There's nothing here.

These stories make use of different stylistic techniques to create a certain impression. The first uses full sentences describing a panoramic scene of the night sky as the character looks up, and in doing so attempts to show the grandeur and wonder of the heavens. The second one, however, uses short, incomplete sentences to establish the main character's discouragement, perhaps even his weariness, as we hear the conversation in his head.

The craft of writing involves understanding and being able to utilize a number of stylistic techniques to create an effect that runs through the entire story.

The techniques fall into three broad categories:

■ **Diction** – Your choice of words and phrases

■ **Narrative drive** – The force that makes a reader feel that something is about to happen

■ **Color** – Vividness of writing through descriptions, imagery and symbolism

Mastering these techniques doesn't mean that your writing will sound like everyone else's. In fact, quite the opposite. Writers who do not master these techniques all tend to sound the same because they put so little effort into ensuring their writing is vibrant and alive.

That's because there are many different ways to make a story dynamic and vigorous...in contrast, there are only a few ways to ensure a story is moribund and gray. Writers who haven't mastered their craft tend to rely on those few ways because they don't know any techniques that'll elevate their storytelling.

You Do It

Read through your short story or a chapter of your novel. Using two different colored pens, mark the passages that lack strong diction, narrative drive and color – and then mark those passages that excel in those three areas.

Step 2. Recognize Mood and Tone

Two ideas closely related to voice are "mood" and "tone."

In every story, the author creates an "emotional atmosphere" – so that a reader might say, "The story felt very solemn" or "The story left me feeling upbeat." The emotional reaction that the story elicits is its mood.

Each story also expresses an "emotional climate" – that is, after completing it the reader might say, "The writer seemed very angry" or "The writer presented a depressing view of the world."

Tone is the emotion the author uses to approach the story's theme.

In a sense, mood is how the story's wording combines to elicit an emotional reaction *from the reader* while tone is the emotional approach *that the author takes*. Consider this passage:

Captain Ashling waved his fist into the air and cheered as his gaze turned skyward to Venus. The planet shined bright as a harbor light. His ship's name would go down in history with the Santa Maria, The Spirit of St. Louis *and the* Eagle.

The paragraph's mood might be described as "exciting" because the reader shares with Captain Ashling his thrill at being given an important mission of exploration. The tone might be described as "uplifting," because the author views exploration as a grand, historical adventure.

Creating mood and tone involve a complex array of techniques that like voice include diction (word choice, sentence structure), narrative drive (pacing), and color (descriptive details).

Mood and tone are not voice, however. Instead, mood and tone are unique to each story whereas voice marks the author's style over several works. Voice is what makes one writer unique from other writers over the course of a career (Though that voice may shift – say be angry in youth but then somber in middle age and finally pensive in old age). In contrast, mood and tone apply more to a specific novel or short story. So an author whose voice tends to be "idealistic" might write one story in which his tone is "utopian" while another story is "optimistic."

You Do It

Read through your short story or chapter. Decide what its mood and tone are. Next, using two different color pens, highlight a few words or passages that first suggest the piece's mood and then the piece's tone. If you can't determine that or find that the piece gives contradictory signals about its mood and tone, this suggests some writing craft issues exist.

Step 3. Strive for Originality

When establishing your voice as a writer, you

want to be original; that is, your plot, characters, setting and ideas should be fresh or novel (no pun intended).

After all, to some degree, you decided to start writing because you had something to tell the world. This need not be some deep philosophical idea but could also be how you say it, such as being able spin the proverbial good yarn. If you started writing to simply retell others' ideas and storylines, you're only being imitative and are not much different than a painter who follows the master's style. You may be skilled at replicating the master's style, but you'll always be in the master's shadow.

Of course, as the old saying goes, "There's nothing new under the sun," so at least to some degree, your story cannot be entirely original. Many genres, for example, have conventions and structures that readers expect.

You also can "borrow" concepts from other writers – sometimes. Ideas or themes always may be used. However, discussing an idea or theme doesn't allow you to use another writer's wording; once you do that, you're guilty of plagiarism.

Further, sometimes terms another writer uses can be borrowed while at other times they can't. The term can be adopted if it's in common usage, like "ray gun" and "space suit"; in fact, several writers have used the same term, and most people who aren't science fiction readers know what they mean. But you're being unoriginal and possibly violating copyright when you use ideas specific to an author or series; for example, "phaser" says "Star Trek" and "ego-likeness" says Frank Herbert's "Dune."

You also can still retell old stories, such as myths, legends and fairy tales. When doing so, however, give it your own sensibility. For example, what makes Robin Hood an interesting character in modern terms? Build on the tale, adding twists to it and making it relevant to modern readers. In addition, when retelling old stories, give it your own voice. For example, you wouldn't tell "King Arthur" using the same diction as Geoffrey of Monmouth.

You Do It

Make a list of your five favorite authors, preferably of fiction. Read your story or novel chapter. Do you see elements of your favorite authors' voice in your writing? While you may emulate their best techniques, be sure to avoid sounding exactly like them.

Diction

A sign of true craftsmanship for a writer is when he selects the right words and arranges them in an evocative way. In this section, you'll learn some techniques – tightening your writing, varying sentence length and structure, using active verbs, and more – to accomplish just that.

Step 4. Identify Elements of Good Diction

The most interesting character facing a significant moral decision in a fast-paced plot and exotic setting will appear bland if the words used are wrong. The vocabulary choices and ways they are arranged to create a sense of style is known as diction.

Consider the diction in this passage:

At first, they thought it was an earthquake. But the ground kept shaking and the dust kept rolling into the scarlet sky, and then came the bellowing of a vast herd. They watched the beasts, which looked vaguely like shaggy triceratops, blunder shoulder-to-shoulder some 30 meters wide over the grassy field in a column that would not end.

Notice how the words describing the event create a sense of terror: the ground doesn't stop shaking, dust is roiling, the sky is a scarlet as opposed to blue, the enormous dinosaur-sized creatures bellow. In fewer than 60 words, the mood is set.

There are many techniques you should keep in mind to improve your writing's diction. They generally fall into five broad categories:

■ **Word choice** – Every word counts when you're writing. The wrong words, for example, can leave a fuzzy impression of a character or scene while others are ambiguous, creating confusion about what is meant. More on this in step

5-11.

■ **Tight writing** – Sometimes unnecessary words are added to a sentence. The result is that the story slows or the scene grays. More on this in Steps 12-15.

■ **Syntax** – A story is not just a collection of well-written sentences. Those sentences must flow together in a rhythm that effectively creates a mood or tone. More on this in Steps 16-17.

■ **Active vs. passive voice** – Related to word choice and tight writing, the verbs you use either can leave you with a story that purrs like an Indy 500 race car or one that sputters like a junker on concrete blocks. More on this in Steps 18-19.

■ **Verb tense** – Whether you tell the story as if it is unfolding before the reader in the present, as would a stage play, or recount events that occur-red in the past, the verb tense you use will alter the pace and the story's readability. More on this in Step 20.

You Do It

Review your story or novel chapter:

■ Are there words in it that are fuzzy or am-biguous? Double underline them.

■ Can a sentence be tightened or written in fewer words? Circle it.

■ Do passages exist where the sentences lack rhy'' n? Draw a line next to it on the side of the

there sentences that use *is, am, are, was,* *being* or *been*? Checkmark those words.

■ Does one sentence tell the story in the present while the next one shifts the story to the past? Underline the two sentences.

Step 5. Aim for Best Word Choice

In any story you tell, your choice of words matters. Selecting the wrong word can lead to a number of problems that quickly turns off the reader to your writing.

Poor word choice results in three general issues: clarity, vagueness and awkwardness.

Clarity

The worse possible outcome of selecting the wrong word will be readers having no idea what you're writing about. That forces them to reread the sentence or passage, which increases the chances that they'll lose track of the storyline. You can be unclear in a number of ways:

■ **Misused words** – Sometimes a similar sounding word is used, as in *Our building is assessable by wheelchair*. The writer really meant *accessible*.

■ **Unwanted connotations or meanings** – Often the reader will laugh at such sentences, for example, *The stowaways knew the only way to stop the pecan truck was to dump the man's nuts all over the road*.

■ **Ambiguity** – *While jogging through the park,*

a dog darted in front of Dawn is confusing because the reader doesn't know if the dog or if Dawn were jogging. More on this in Step 11.

■ **Subjective tension** – If you wrote *He raised his eyes*, you wouldn't literally mean that the character moved higher on his forehead, but the wrong word choice here creates a difference between what you've written and what you wanted to say. More on this in Step 7.

■ **Jargon/technical terms** – Unless the reader is a bicycle repairman, *Because the fork had a negative air chamber, Tony removed the cover cap from the bottom left fork leg* will make little sense.

Vagueness

Using inexact and fuzzy words leads to bland sentences that fail to create a vivid picture of what is occurring. For example: *She seemed really tall.*

Words like *seemed* and *really* don't give the reader a detailed enough picture of the scene or character. Was she tall or not? And if she was tall, then just how high was she? More on this in Steps 9 and 10.

Awkwardness

Sentences become difficult to understand because using the wrong word forces a writer to create structures that make little sense. This almost always results in a sentence lacking rhythm. For example: *My buddies were anticipating more than their dates.*

The writer means to say that his buddies are feeling a greater sense of anticipation than their dates. That makes *anticipating more* a poor word choice.

To correct it, a different form of the words *anticipating more* needs to be used and the sentence should be slightly restructured, perhaps as, *My buddies expressed a greater sense of anticipation than their dates.*

You Do It

Look at the words you double underlined in Step 4. Correct those word choices that lead to misused words, unwanted connotations or meanings, jargon and awkwardness.

Step 6. Avoid Clever-Author Syndrome

When we've mastered some skill – say ball handling in basketball – we often like to show off. So when we're on the sidewalk with the neighbor kids, we'll spin the ball on a finger or perform some gravity-defying dribbling trick.

When writers resort to such showing off in a story, they're guilty of clever-author syndrome. A term coined by Cambridge Science Fiction Workshop's David Smith, clever-author syndrome occurs when a writer uses literary razzle dazzle not to advance the story but just to show us that he's really smart.

For example, you might use unnecessarily large words that the majority of your readers never would know. Or you might make obscure references. Or you might be guilty of purple prose.

Just as a basketball player wouldn't show off in a game to demonstrate he's a great ball handler (the Harlem Globetrotters aside), so a writer shouldn't show off in a story just to demonstrate he's clever. In both cases, it's vanity rather than focusing on what really matters: winning the game for the basketball player – or advancing the story for the writer.

You Do It

Look at words you double underlined in Step 4. Delete passages in which you're guilty of clever author syndrome.

Step 7. Erase Subjective Tension

When our word choice is so off that it causes readers to laugh (or at least groan), you're probably committing the error of "subjective tension." This is "the difference between what you mean and what you actually say," an apt phrase coined by science fiction writer Samuel R. Delany.

Usually this difference amounts to something that is humorous or campy, which can break the tone of your piece. Some examples include:

■ *Her jaw fell to the floor.*

■ *He jumped through the door.*

■ *She strained her eyes as looking through the window.*

■ *He twisted up his face.*

Of course, none of these images literally can occur. Hence, the suspension of disbelief that a reader brings to a story is broken.

A variant of subjective tension is the gag detail, which is "an unnecessarily unrealistic detail that blows the story's credibility," according to CSFW member Sarah Smith, who devised the term. An example of a gag detail she gives is, "I can accept a Neanderthal going to Harvard, but a Neanderthal with a middle name? Gag."

Sometimes, though, subjective tension and gag details can be used to great effect. They can help form the repertoire of jokes in a humorous story, as in Douglas Adams' "The Hitchhiker's Guide to the Galaxy." If done right and maintained throughout the entire piece, they can create a deliberately campy and fun story, such as the 1960s "Batman" television series.

You Do It

Look at words you double underlined in Step 4, rewriting and possibly even deleting any examples of subjective tension or gag details – unless you are writing comedy, of course (In that case, see if there are spots you might add them!).

Step 8. Murder Your Darlings

To engage your readers – whether writing fiction or nonfiction – you'll need to be utterly ruthless with your own words. In short, you'll need to "murder your darlings."

You've probably heard the axiom before. Though promoted by science fiction writer James Patrick Kelly, the advice is often given to writers of all genres – and for good reason.

Here's the problem: Writers fall in love with their words. Like their own children or lovers, a writer's words can do no wrong. And if they do, the transgression is highly forgivable given the surrounding words' beauty.

But some words in our stories are "precious freeloaders who are too busy looking good to do any work," as Kelly points out. He recommends eliminating those words, or to "murder your darlings."

(A side note here: The phrase actually is borrowed from Sir Arthur Quiller-Couch, who wrote, "Whenever you feel an impulse to perpetrate a piece of exceptionally fine writing, obey it – wholeheartedly – and delete it before sending your manuscript to press. Murder your darlings." But really, who remembers Sir Arthur Quiller-Couch?)

Such freeloading words actually slow your story. They distract from the action, which in turn keeps readers from remaining focused on how your main character faces his central problem – and that latter conflict, after all, is the heart of the traditional story.

Beginning writers often make the mistake of trying to fix wordiness by adding words rather than cutting them. Yet, that's like adding more fatty meat to the plate rather than trimming the cut you've already got. For a proper, attractive presentation, trim the fat already there.

What are some darlings that ought to be excised? Kelly identifies six "darlings" that can be killed:

■ **Adjectival and adverbial leeches** – Descriptive words should be selected very carefully. They ought to create atmosphere and offer insights into the character, not decorate a paragraph.

■ **Clumsy entrances and exits** – Too often stories contain "here to there" action that shows how a character got from one place to another. Providing that info typically is irrelevant to the story.

■ **Unnecessary scene or time switches** – Many stories can take place in a couple of locations or during the course of a few hours. Switching the when and where of a story often forces you to waste words to re-establish the setting and mood as well as explaining why the change occurred.

■ **Overpopulation (extra characters)** – Limit a story (especially short stories and novellas) to a few characters – the main character, the villain, the sidekick, a couple of background characters. Each additional character requires some description and takes attention away from the main character.

■ **Overdramatization (too much "show" and not enough "tell")** – In fiction, exposition kills a story. If readers wanted to read an encyclopedia, they would have grabbed a Compton's from the bookshelf, not your book. More on this in Step 25.

■ **Arriving early, staying late** – When and where stories and scenes start and end is vital. Think of "The Iliad": Homer doesn't begin with the war's start 10 years earlier but begins the tale in the days leading up to the final battle.

You Do It
With manuscript in hand, take out your red pen knife and murder your darlings.

Step 9. Replace Fuzzy Words

To really improve your writing, your words should be very specific and read maybe something like what you'd find in a story that's not loosely written.

Huh?

The problem with the above advice is it's riddled with fuzzy words – or words that aren't precise: *really, very, maybe, something like, not so loosely.*

Such words weaken your writing by giving an inexact, out-of-focus picture of the landscape or idea that you're portraying.

Other fuzzy words include *almost, half-, very, really, seem, looked like,* and *felt.*

They're also known as "weasel words," because as a writer, you have a responsibility to be precise.

By using fuzzy words, though, the writer fails to do the hard work of writing and instead behaves like an optometrist who does a sloppy job and hands a customer a pair of glasses in which the prescription is wrong.

The opening sentence would be improved if rewritten as: To improve your writing, your words should be specific, like those in a tightly-constructed story.

As with any rule, there's an exception, of course.

Fuzzy words might be used in dialogue to show that a character has an imprecise sense of what occurred (*"I only got a glimpse – it looked to be almost eight feet tall."*) or when that character is being deceptive (*He suppressed a grimace. "It's very good," he said, not looking up.*).

You Do It

Look at the words you double underlined in Step 4.

Delete or replace any fuzzy words in your manuscript with words that are precise.

Step 10. Tell Readers What 'It' Is

Avoid starting sentences – and especially paragraphs – with "it."

By starting a sentence with "it," you can confuse the reader. After all, what exactly does "it" refer to?

The previous sentence should specifically give the word that "it" clearly refers to. For example: *Ask him out for dinner. Then pay for it.* In this case, *it* clearly refers to *dinner.*

If this doesn't occur, you'll want to restructure the sentence.

In addition, starting sentences with "it" usually means you're using passive voice. Typically the word "is" follows "it," as in *It's very stressful for a relationship to survive in circumstances such as this.*

Starting a sentence with "it" rarely is the tightest of writing. The sentence probably can be shortened. For example, *It took a lot of hard work and a lot of luck in matching up two people, but it was done* could be rewritten as *A lot of hard work and luck was needed to match up two people, but it was done.* The second sentence is three words shorter and easier to read.

To rewrite a sentence that starts with "it," ask yourself what "it" refers to. The answer is what should be used in place of "it" in your sentence. To wit, in *It's relatively inexpensive to get a back-*

ground check and will put your mind at ease, "it" really is *getting a background check.*

Next, replace "it" with your answer (and clean up the rest of the sentence), so that you have *Getting a background check is relatively expensive and will put your mind at ease.* You still have passive voice, but the sentence is tighter and clearer.

An exception to this rule is dialogue. People naturally misuse "it" when speaking, and to make dialogue appear realistic, you may want to have a character start a sentence with "it."

This generally is a good idea for characters trying to figure out something about themselves or another, as starting a sentence with "it" suggests that their thoughts are still nebulous and unclear, as in, *It may have been the murder weapon.*

You Do It

Look at each instance "it" is used in your manuscript. Can you tell what "it" is?

If not, rewrite the sentence so that "it" does not appear.

Step 11. Eliminate Ambiguity

Sometimes when writing, we unintentionally create ambiguity – that is, we write a sentence that can be interpreted in more than one way.

You've probably ran into this when reading instructions for a do-it-yourself kit or when trying to resolve some technical issue with your computer. For example: *Put one button at another button.*

Exactly what does that mean? How do you place a button "at" another button? Does one go on top of the other or next to it? Is one button moved and then replaced by the other button?

In fiction, usually the result is that one of the interpretations is humorous, which distracts the reader from focusing on the story, as it breaks the suspension of disbelief. For example:

She stood and cleaned up her glass and napkin.

Did she literally take a wash cloth to her glass and napkin or did she bring them to the kitchen sink and trash can?

Often as writers we're too close to the text to realize that a line is ambiguous. We know in our heads what we're trying to say and so see only that when reading a line.

To identify ambiguities, look for the couple of common grammar problems that often lead to them.

The first is pronoun references. In the sentence *Jenny told Sandra that she was mistaken*, the reader doesn't know which one Jenny believes is mistaken – herself or Sandra. It could simply be rewritten as *"I'm mistaken," Jenny told Sandra* or *"You're mistaken," Jenny said.*

A second is dangling modifiers. For example, *While hiking through the mountains, a boulder rolled in front of Kris* suggests that the boulder was hiking through the woods because the modifier *While hiking through the woods* is misplaced.

Instead, restructure the sentence so that it reads *While Kris hiked through the mountains, a boulder rolled in front of her.*

By eliminating ambiguities, we make our writing more concise.

You Do It
Read through your manuscript and eliminate all of the confusing pronoun references, dangling modifiers, and other ambiguities.

Step 12. Ditch the Begin Fallacy

To keep up a story's pace – and hence the reader's interest – you'll want to write as tightly as possible. Metaphorically, you'll squeeze all you can from your words so that a sentence is as compact as possible with no extra, unnecessary words spilling out.

One way to achieve that is to eliminate the begin fallacy. This occurs when the writer introduces an action to the reader by saying *began to*, as in *My nerves began to calm.*

The writer can cut *began to*, however, and tighten the wording by saying, *My nerves calmed.* Notice how it's not only a shorter sentence but a stronger one because *calmed* is the main verb rather than *began*.

You Do It
Delete begin fallacies from your manuscript.

Step 13. Stop Weighing Down Passages with Adverbs

Does a passage you've written feel weighed down? Perhaps it sounds pretty but doesn't have any *oomph*? Your problem might be an overuse of adverbs.

Adverbs are words that typically describe a verb (Though they also can describe adjectives and other adverbs, which can be a symptom of a bloated passage.). For example, in the sentence *He walked quickly across the deck*, "quickly" is an adverb because it describes or modifies *walked,* the verb.

The sentence could be tightened by dumping *quickly walked* and replacing it with a stronger verb. *Strode* – which indicates a brisk walk – might work better. The sentence then would read, *He strode across the deck.*

If you've got a lot of adverbs in a passage, you're probably relying too much on that part of speech to do the hard work in your sentence. Adverbs, however, aren't the muscle that an exact verb provides. While you may need to use an adverb on occasion, our language generally is broad enough that you can find the right verb.

So trim the fat in your writing and build a buff sentence capable of delivering a right hook to your reader. Or as Strunk and White famously advised with another metaphor, remember that "an adverb is a leech sucking the strength from a verb."

You Do It

Look at the sentences you circled in Step 4. Get rid of any adverbial leeches.

Step 14. Improve Writing's Texture by Avoiding Repetition

One of the quickest ways to ruin a story's texture is to repeat the same word between sentences and paragraphs. For example:

Koorana quivered as Birray's scent grew stronger than ever before, so strong that the teenager thought it entwined with her very blood. For a teenage male with such wide shoulders, he possessed the sweetest smile, she mused, and so tall, too. He motioned to look up, and Koorana realized everyone else in the tent was standing. She broke her stare, quickly stood. Averting her eyes to the dirt ground beneath them, Koorana vowed to concentrate on the service, but a moment later she allowed herself one last look at Birray. He was still staring at her and winked. The teenager turned back, happy, and even in the dim light could see the flowers adorning the altar.

Notice how some words, particularly *teenager* and its variant *teenage,* are repeated? The paragraph could be improved by eliminating two of the three uses of that word, perhaps by replacing the first *teenager* with a synonym such as *adolescent* and simply using the pronoun *she* for *The teenager* in the last sentence.

Gustave Flaubert recommended never using a word more than once on a single page, but that's probably a bit extreme. After all, sometimes repeating the word is necessary for rhetorical effect. Consider this passage:

"Do you realize how complex living things are?" the gobena said from the revival's dais. The crowd's eyes clung to him despite the heat exacerbated by the tent walls' dark hadrosaur hide. "Do you realize how complex a family is, with all of its interactions and behaviors? But some say life is no more difficult to make than the simple whistles of an ugly scrubfowl."

The audience laughed.

"How could organs as complicated as the eye or the ear or the brain of even a tiny bird ever come about by chance or natural processes?" the gobena continued. "How could a family?"

The gobena's speech harkens to that of a revivalist and thus seems more real when the phrases *Do you realize how complex* and *How could* are repeated.

Another acceptable practice for repetition is

when using an invisible word, like *the, and* or *said*. In the preceding passage, *the* was used 11 times, though you probably didn't notice it.

Beyond these instances, however, avoiding repetition of words is advisable.

You Do It

Rewrite sentences in your manuscript that repeat words within them or that were used in a previous sentence.

Step 15. Eschew Clichés Like a Toxic Waste Dump

A quick way to strengthen your writing is to replace (or just avoid altogether) overused expressions and phrases. These expressions and phrases are known as clichés. They include terms such as *avoid like the plague, beat around the bush,* or *kiss of death.*

Such expressions are so overused that they've lost their force. While most readers understand the point being made by a cliché, few understand the origin of and meaning behind the expression. In addition, because of their overuse, clichés sound trite.

Rather than rely on clichés, writers who've mastered their craft develop more clever ways of conveying an idea or feeling. These clever expressions delight readers. After all, part of the fun of reading is seeing how writers play with words.

Putting them together in unique, evocative ways isn't just fun for the reader – it's part of the joy of writing.

Some common clichés include: a matter of time, as old as the hills, brave as a lion, every cloud has a silver lining, fall head over heels, in the nick of time, like the plague, nerves of steel, read between the lines, scared out of my wits, the quiet before the storm, the writing on the wall, time will tell, without a care in the world

You Do It

Rewrite any clichés in your manuscript. This can be done by thinking of an analogy for the cliché. For example, instead of *airing dirty laundry,* you might say, *He dumped a trash can full of his problems over me.*

Step 16. Vary Syntax to Give Writing Flavor, Texture

When writing, you'll want to vary the syntax, which is the pattern of the sentence's words – that is, the order of the parts of speech within a sentence.

A standard sentence pattern in English is the Subject-Verb-Direct Object, as in *Aunt Janie sewed the button on my shirt,* in which *Aunt Janie* is the Subject (or who the sentence is about), *sewed* is the Verb (or tells what the Subject did), and *the button on my shirt* is the Direct Object (or who the

Subject did the Verb to).

But an English sentence can be structured a number of different ways. For example, you might use a Verb-Subject pattern, as in *Run Shelly!* in which *Run* is the Verb (or what the Subject should do) and *Shelly* is the Subject (or who the sentence is about).

If you don't vary your syntax, the writing will sound stilted. In addition, your sentences will be about the same length, resulting in paragraphs that sound monotone. It would be like ordering a banana split but getting a big bowl of only vanilla ice cream. Varying the syntax adds flavor and texture to your writing.

Because of the English language's grammar, most of your sentences will be S-V-DO. But placing modifiers in different locations of the sentence can add textual variety. For example, you could write *Concentrating on the work before her, Aunt Janie sewed the button on my shirt* in which *Concentrating on the work before her* is a modifier showing how *Aunt Janie* (the Subject) is sewing.

Of course, there are times when you may not want to vary the sentence structure. One is for rhetorical effect. Consider these lines from Martin Luther King Jr.'s famous "I Have a Dream" speech:

I have a dream that one day this nation will rise up and live out the true meaning of its creed: "We hold these truths to be self-evident: that all men are created equal."

I have a dream that one day on the red hills of Georgia the sons of former slaves and the sons of former slave owners will be able to sit down to-gether at the table of brotherhood.

I have a dream that one day even the state of Mississippi, a state sweltering with the heat of in-justice, sweltering with the heat of oppression, will be transformed into an oasis of freedom and jus-tice.

I have a dream that my four little children will one day live in a nation where they will not be judged by the color of their skin but by the content of their character.

The reason those lines work despite the un-varying sentence structure is because by repeat-ing certain key words and the same sentence structure, they have a rhythm to them, much like a poem or song lyric. Just as importantly, the wording in the sentences evoke powerful images that tap into our emotions and humanity.

Another instance in which you may wish to re-peat the same sentence structure is when devel-oping a character. If you wish to show that the character has a dull personality, perhaps that per-son will speak this way. Don't overdo it, though, as after a while this can grate on a reader.

You Do It

Look at the passages that you drew a line next to in Step 4. Vary the sentence structure used in these sections.

Of course, if the sentence does not vary because you're aiming for a rhetorical effect, read it to en-sure you have parallel constructions.

Step 17. Scour Fragments from Your Writing

Should you use fragments in your writing? Your high school English teacher almost certainly said "No!" and marked it with a red pen.

Fragments are okay if they serve a rhetorical effect, such as when creating suspense. For example: *She realized something was behind her. Something large. Something breathing heavily.*

Still, fragments should be used sparingly. For a rhetorical effect to be successful, it needs to stand out from the rest of the text. It can't do that if used frequently.

Fragments need revising if they don't really serve this effect or if they are confusing to understand because they aren't a complete sentence.

You Do It

Convert unnecessary fragments in your manuscript to complete sentences. This might be done by adding words to the fragment so that you have a complete sentence or by combining the fragment with an adjoining sentence. In a few instances, you might simply delete the fragment.

Step 18. Turn Passive Passages into Active Voice

So you've written a scene packed with action,

ripe with conflict, and filled with tension – but every time you read it, the writing feels flat. The problem may be that you're writing in passive rather than active voice.

Active voice is when the subject of the sentence does (or acts upon) something. In the following active voice sentence, the subject (streak of light), does something (arcs):

The streak of light arced across the sky as if a falling star.

Passive voice, however, occurs when the subject is acted upon. For example, the above sentence in passive voice would be written as:

Arcing across the sky, as if a falling star, was a streak of light.

Passive voice generally should be avoided, for a couple of reasons:

■ **It's dull** – It's like telling you something "exists." In the above example, the author really is saying *In the sky exists a streak of light.* Sleeker and more economical, active voice speeds up the story.

■ **It's awkward** – Notice how the phrase *as if a falling star* seems stuck in the middle of the sentence, as if it is out of place. Rewriting the sentence so it's in active voice would give the phrase a place to fit.

■ **It's wordy** – The passive voice sentence above says in 14 words what the active voice sentence says in 13 words. One word may not seem like much, but in a 100,000-word novel, it can mean a few unnecessary pages of copy.

Of course, sometimes passive voice is ne ... You do need, on occasion, to tell people that something "exists," especially when writing exposition. In addition, you don't want to overdo it with active voice. The reader can only go at high speed so long before getting motion sickness.

How do you know if you have a passive voice sentence? Look for being verbs – these are verbs that show the subject *exists*. There are only eight being verbs: *is, are, am, was, were, be, being* and *been*. Also, look for the three words *had, has* and *have,* which are week fill-ins for the verb *possess.* If any of those words appear in your sentence, you need an active verb.

Converting passive to active voice is a simple process. First, identify the sentence's subject, or who/what the sentence is doing something. For example, in the passive sentence *Through him was running an icy shiver,* "shiver" is the subject.

Next, place the subject at the sentence's beginning. You would then have a sentence that reads *An icy shiver through him was running.*

Then identify the verb, or the words that describe what the subject is doing. In this case, it's *was running.* Place those words immediately after the subject so that the sentence now reads, *An icy shiver was running through him.*

Finally, get economical by cutting out the being words – in this case *was* – and reworking the verb so it makes sense in the sentence. The sentence we're working on now would read *An icy shiver ran through him.*

You now have a sentence in active voice.

Sometimes you may have to replace the being verb with an active voice verb that actually shows action. For example, in the passive sentence *Miles of salt flats, a dry bed of crimson and pastel green, is between them,* "is" needs to be replaced with a verb. *Separated* would work much better. The sentence *Miles of salt flats, a dry bed of crimson and pastel green, separated them* is in active voice.

You Do It

Look at the being verbs you checkmarked in Step 4. Rewrite those sentences so that they are in active voice.

Step 19. Spunk up Your Writing: Replace Overused Verbs

Even when using active verbs, sentences still may sound flat. More than likely, those active verbs are also overused.

An overused verb is one that's commonplace and dull. Among the many active verbs that tend to be used to excess in our daily language and writing are *sat, looked for, felt, enjoy, gave* and *became.*

Relying on such commonplace verbs amounts to inefficient writing and hence inefficient storytelling. Such words don't give you the most value for your writing dollar.

Instead, invest in verbs that reveal mood. For example, replace a word like *sat* with *slumped* or *flopped*.

You Do It

Locate overused verbs in your manuscript. Come up with stronger verbs, especially ones that reveal mood, to replace them.

Step 20. Watch for Verb Tense Shifts

A common mistake among novice writers is shifting within their story so that events occurred in the now but then in the next paragraph happen in the past. This is a sign that the writer is changing verb tenses.

There are two common verb tenses in which you could write. Most typically used is *past tense*. In this case, the story's events are told as if they've happened in the past (never mind that your story may be set in the future – the reader actually is hearing about the events from a future beyond which the story is told):

Col. Noel turned away from the reflection of his wrinkled face in the starcraft's portal. Nothing to see but dust and gas anyway, he muttered to himself. His baggy eyes glanced at the gamma ray radiation sensors; soon the ship would enter the glowing cloud's open center, where immortality awaited him. He moved toward the helm but cringed as the arthritis in his knee spiked. There was nanomedicine for the infirmity, but taking the capsules only reminded him of his body's inevitable slow destruction. He sighed, resorted to giving the computer a voice command to slow speed, noticed a rasp in his words that had never been there before.

The other verb tense used in stories is *present tense*. In this case, the story's events unfold exactly at the same time that the reader reads them. Notice how the above example of past tense writing changes when rewritten in present tense:

Col. Noel turns away from the reflection of his wrinkled face in the starcraft's portal. Nothing to see but dust and gas anyway, he mutters to himself. His baggy eyes glance at the gamma ray radiation sensors; soon the ship will enter the glowing cloud's open center, where immortality awaits him. He moves toward the helm but cringes as the arthritis in his knee spikes. There was nanomedicine for the infirmity, but taking the capsules only reminds him of his body's inevitable slow destruction. He sighs, resorts to giving the computer a voice command to slow speed, notices a rasp in his words that had never been there before.

Writers should stick to one tense. Shifting between tenses jars the reader.

In addition, writers rarely should use present tense. In the hands of a master, such as Margaret Atwood in her novel "The Handmaid's Tale," it can be used to great effect by creating a sense of immediacy and making the narrators' voice unique. But present tense largely is an unnatural way of telling a story. After all, which of the two versions of Col. Noel's tale do you prefer?

You Do It

Look at the sentences you underlined in Step 4. Rewrite them in past tense. If adamant about telling your story in present tense (Sometimes stories do work better in that tense.), then revise any past tense passages, ensuring they are in present tense. Either way, your goal is to tell a story using only one verb tense.

Narrative Drive

Ever read a story before bed and find it so gripping that you stay up far later than you should just to find out what is going to happen? If so, you've been a "victim" of narrative drive. Narrative drive is the force that makes a reader feel that something is about to happen. The more powerful your narrative drive, the less likely the reader is to put down the story. During the sections ahead, we'll examine what gives a story great narrative drive – and what detracts from it.

Step 21. Give Your Story *Oomph!* with Narrative Drive

All of the great works of literature have powerful narrative drives.

But creating a strong narrative drive involves a lot more than devising interesting worlds as does Frank Herbert in "Dune," an intriguing main character as does Orson Scott Card in "Ender's Game," or a fascinating premise as does Isaac Asimov in "Foundation." It is all of these things and more: good plotting, mesmerizing settings, captivating characters, proper point of view selection, an absorbing theme, and an artists' handling of stylistic issues. So, while books or instructors may discuss elements of a story in isolation, always remember that a good story is the sum of these parts.

To obtain narrative drive then requires a full sense of a story's various elements. Still, there are a couple of things to keep in mind to improve your story's narrative drive:

■ **Link description with action** – Whenever you opt to describe a landscape or character, ensure that it serves the dual purpose of moving the story's plot forward. For example, to emphasize the difficulty of a journey, you might describe the bleakness of the desert landscape that our main character finds himself in. Writing *The sun shined* *down from a clear blue sky*, however, does little to create a sense of danger in the same setting. We'll cover more on this later, beginning with Step 37.

■ **Avoid stiff writing by using repetitious and superfluous wording** – Poor writing follows a "He did this then this happened" pattern while quality writing takes an "As he did this, this happened" approach. *Aunt Mildred picked up the hot bowl from the counter. She dropped the bowl, spilling the mashed potatoes all over the floor* takes the "He did this then this happened" approach; it's wordy and slow-paced. *As Aunt Mildred picked up the hot bowl, it slipped from her fingers, spilling mashed potatoes all over the floor* takes the "As he did this, this happened" approach; it's fast-paced and efficient in word count.

You Do It

Review your manuscript for lines that follow a "He did this then this happened" approach. Rewrite them so they follow an "As he did this, this happened" style.

Step 22. Sustain Dramatic Tension through Good Pacing

As developing your story, maintaining a sense of tension is vital. Without dramatic tension – a feeling of uncertainty in the reader about how the main character will solve (or even if he will re-solve) the central problem – the story will be flat and vanilla.

Creating tension involves controlling the story's pace. Pace is the timing by which the major events in the plot unfold and in which the big scenes are shown.

The "better" the story, then the better that the author handled the pace. Douglas Adams' comedic novel "The Hitchhiker's Guide to the Galaxy" and Ray Bradbury's short story "A Sound of Thunder," though done in quite different tones, both are examples of masterful pacing.

Every story has a different pace. Those that are more introspective tend to move at a slower pace while those that are action-packed tend to be fast. Because of this, all stories run on a "story clock." This is a measurement in which action is internally described. As with the wider universe, however, there is no objective clock. A true sign of craftsmanship is when an author sets the story clock winding at the right pace for an individual tale.

Regardless of the story, however, good pacing always involves compression and expansion of time – In a story, events don't unfold at the same rate as they do in real time. For example, a suborbital flight from New York to Tokyo in real time might take an hour, but in the story it's handled in a phrase that takes a couple of seconds to read. Usually the author speeds up or slows down the action to match the emotions he wants the reader to have.

Another aspect of good pacing is "travel time." Characters don't change their personalities or their minds about important decisions overnight. A character must "travel" a certain emotional distance to arrive at such changes. The author's wording and dramatic action must mirror that pace.

Of course, you have only so many words to tell a story, so reducing that "travel time" is important.

There are a few ways you can accomplish that without cheating on the emotional distance that a character must traverse:

■ **Intercut a different story** – Sometimes a parallel story or subplot can help lead the character to change more quickly because he realizes, through analogy, that he must change.

■ **Fill intervening time with straight action** – A change often doesn't occur because one has thought through a problem but because physical experiences test and uncover what one truly believes. Straight action can be a crucible that helps the character come to a new understanding.

■ **Develop other characters** – As with a parallel story or subplot, other characters who undergo change can affect the protagonist. Their changes can test and alter the protagonist's beliefs.

■ **Offer description** – Changes in the landscape and climate can symbolically represent the emotional currents in the protagonist's thinking.

You Do It

Review your manuscript for pacing. Mark scenes that move slow (especially ones suffering from travel time) and those that move too fast. Rewrite those scenes to improve the pacing.

Step 23. Create an Uncertain Outcome for Your Main Character

If your story feels flat, you may want to look at the plot and ask yourself, "Do my readers have a sense of anticipation yet uncertainty about what will come next?"

If the answer is "No," then your story lacks suspense.

"Suspense" is difficult to define if only because there are so many different thoughts about exactly what it is. Further, suspense for one genre, such as a mystery story, may be more subdued than in others, such as a western or science fiction tale.

At its core, though, suspense in any genre occurs when the outcome for the main character is uncertain. The more a reader is invested in finding out the answer to that uncertainty, the more suspenseful the story. In large part, suspense is enhanced by the building of tension.

Writers can develop suspense in a number of ways:

■ **Create characters with problems** – If your main character has no central problem to solve or has no motive for solving it, you don't have much of a story. Deepen the suspense by giving the main character good reason to be resistant to resolving the story's central problem.

■ **Withhold the hidden story** – As a writer, you know the full backstory of your characters and how the plot will unfold. Don't spill that to readers. Divulge it in small portions, and only when necessary to further the plot.

■ **Hide characters' motives from one another** – While readers need to know why your main character behaves a certain way, other characters don't need to know that. Your main character then doesn't understand why other characters act as they do, and this inexplicable behavior can lead to conflict between them.

■ **Employ the Hitchcock Effect** – Movie master Alfred Hitchcock allowed the audience, through a character's dialogue and scenery shots, to infer a danger. Whether or not the character then might step into that dangerous situation creates suspense.

■ **Add some action** – If your main character has nothing to do, then there are no problems to resolve, and the story quickly loses momentum (Of course, the classic "Waiting for Godot" has virtually no action, but the author utilizes other methods of creating suspense to make up for this.). All action should have a point to it, however; mainly, it needs to impel the main character to resolve the story's central problem.

You Do It

Does your manuscript's main character face an uncertain outcome? If not, then utilize one (or more) of the above techniques to ramp up the story's suspense.

Step 24. Generate Tension by Leaving Reader in Doubt

Any story you tell by definition has a plot, characters, setting, point of view and theme. But to really make a story pop, an author has to interweave and play these elements against one another so that the story has tension.

Tension is the force behind the need to find resolution. It stems from the hook that caught the reader in the opening lines, that there's an interesting central problem to solve. The rest of the story needs to focus on solving that problem.

But the author can't make the outcome – the resolution of the problem – obvious to the reader. The author should always leave open the possibility that the problem won't be resolved. Of course, most readers know (or at least expect) that the problem will be resolved. By creating doubt, the writer causes the reader to wonder how the problem will be resolved. The greater this tension, the more likely the reader will stick with you through the story.

Generally, the best way to create doubt is to make the problem increasingly more difficult to resolve as the story continues.

Consider the tension created in what is perhaps the best "Star Trek: The Next Generation" episode, "The Best of Both Worlds, Part I." The show opens with attacks on a Federation outpost and ship that indicates a Borg invasion. Great anxiety ensues as Starfleet Command hastily organizes an armada while its own leaders admit they're not ready for the Borg. The problem worsens as the *Enterprise* engages the Borg, begins to lose the battle and hides in a nebula. The Borg force the *Enterprise* out and abduct Captain Picard, leaving the crew in the hands of Commander Riker, who is doubtful of his own leadership abilities and finds himself at odds with the Borg expert, Lt. Cmdr. Shelby. Though the *Enterprise* is able to temporarily halt the Borg advance, an away team sent to retrieve Picard finds that he has been transformed into a Borg. As the away team reports this to Riker, Picard – as Locutus of Borg – orders the *Enterprise* to surrender, saying that everything Picard knows the Borg now know and that resistance is futile. Riker orders the *Enterprise* to fire, or for the crew to kill its beloved, former captain.

The story constantly leaves the viewer wondering how the *Enterprise*/Federation will overcome the Borg invasion as the situation for our heroes grows increasingly dire. By episode's end (which was a season cliffhanger), apparently the only way to resolve the problem is for the crew to kill the series' main character and hero, the man they are most loyal to.

Certainly the story's settings – aboard the Borg ship, on a world where a colony has been decimated – are intriguing. Certainly the characters – Riker's self-doubt, Picard's transformation into Locutus – are fascinating. Certainly the plot – repelling an alien invasion – is interesting. But combining and playing these elements off against one another to create tension – now that's spellbinding.

You Do It

Are there sections of your manuscript in which the reader is *not* left in doubt about the story's outcome? If these sections come before the story's climax, consider revising them to create dramatic tension.

Step 25. Show, Don't Tell

Want to slow your story to a glacial grind and get readers to quit reading your story? Then load it with lots of exposition.

Indeed, problems arising with exposition often (and rightfully) elicit cries of "Show, don't tell!" from editors.

Exposition is directly conveying information to the reader. For example, you could write, *She found herself falling in love him.* You've directly told the reader what is occurring to the main character: she's falling in love.

A better way to tell that she's falling in love is to show it. Instead write: *Birray took her in his arms. She nestled her head against his chest as he caressed her back.* That she nestled her head against his chest, in the context of the rest of the story, will show she's beginning to have stronger than "just friends" feelings for him.

Why avoid exposition? Three good reasons:

■ **It slows the forward movement of plot** – As exposition amounts to straightforward information, some novice writers believe it speeds up the story. In truth, it robs the story of conflict and tension. Showing rather than telling what happens allows the reader to see incrementally how a character is pulled and dragged into feeling a certain way or making a specific decision.

■ **It amounts to lecturing the reader or forcing him to read an encyclopedia entry** – A lot of times exposition is background information that the author deems is important to understanding some concept, such as the history of the Clone Wars, the physics behind hyperdrive, and the ethical dilemmas of using metagenic weapons. It's better to sprinkle these matters as bits into the characters' normal conversation rather than give a long lecture.

■ **It can violate viewpoint** – A first-person story suddenly interrupted with an objective, third-person telling of exposition can be jarring to the tale's flow. At the very least, it is awkward-sounding.

You Do It

Find spots in your manuscript where you show rather than tell. Rewrite those sentences so that they infer rather than directly state an emotion or reaction. Here's an online explanation of how to do just that: inventingrealityeditingservice.type pad.com/inventing_reality_editing/2013/0/ how-to-make-your-writing-show-rather-than-tell.html.

Step 26. Step Down on Authorisms

Sometimes when writers just can't think of what to put on the page, they resort to an inappropriate technique known as an authorism.

An authorism – coined by American writer Thomas M. Disch – occurs when the writer places his or her physical environment, mannerisms and prejudices into the story.

For example, while thinking of how to pace a scene, the author pours herself a cup of coffee. In the story, the character then also pours a cup of coffee.

The problem with an authorism is that the character may have absolutely no reason to pour a cup of coffee as far as the story is concerned. She might, of course, be trying to avoid a person who is talking to her and so turns away and uses the pouring of a cup of coffee as an excuse to not look at him. Possibly the pouring of the cup of coffee is part of the description intended to show the reader that the character has just awakened.

But where an authorism is concerned, there's no point to the action.

You want to excise all wordage that serves no use in a story. Including it only slows the piece and drains its vitality.

You may get lucky in that an authorism is not always apparent to readers. But they will sense the poor pacing and think less of the story for it.

A reader may just give up on the story, though, if the authorism is extremely obtrusive. For example, the character starts a scene by staring at a blank wall (a metaphor for staring at a blank page) or even worse complains that they don't know what to do (a metaphor for the author not knowing what to write).

You Do It

Delete any authorisms in your story. You probably do not want to rewrite them as dialogue in the story. Instead, your story should infer your message or theme, which you will if your characters' actions make the case for it.

Step 27. Strike out Nulls

Sometimes the only purpose of a story's sentence is to say that nothing happened. Such sentences are called "nulls." An example would be the sentence *He said nothing.* Fortunately, nulls are easy to spot: If your story were occurring in real life, nulls would be the points where nothing happens.

Nulls can be deleted from the story. They almost always reduce the piece's immediacy and dramatic tension.

You Do It

Identify and cross out any nulls in your manuscript. Then read the edited passages – do you see how the story's pace speeds up?

Step 28. Cut Card Tricks in the Dark

No one likes a show off. Unfortunately, one way novice writers slow their story is by saying "Look see what I can do!" When they use such authorial cleverness for no purpose other than to show off, they're guilty of using card tricks in the dark," a term coined by American science fiction writer Lewis Shiner.

A common example of "card tricks in the dark includes a humorous scene that has no point other than to be humorous. And it probably does elicit laughs because it is humorous. But the scene – like every other word, sentence and paragraph the author has written in the story –

ought to have a dramatic payoff.

A humorous scene might offer a dramatic payoff by relieving tension. Shakespeare does this when he inserts the humorous monologue of a drunken porter into "Macbeth." That provides dramatic payoff because the audience then does not become numb to the deaths and violence unfolding in the play. The monologue offers the added benefit of advancing the play's theme.

Or a humorous scene might help establish the characters' motivations and personalities. The kind of jokes a character tells and how the characters react to it tells a great amount about them. However, once that's been established, there's not much need to keep doing this with humorous scene after humorous scene.

You Do It

Delete or rewrite any scenes that show off your writing skills (such as writing humor) but in no way advance the plot or develop the characters.

Step 29. Avoid Handwaving to Cover Story Flaw

Sometimes when a car salesman has a shoddy vehicle to sell, he tries to distract you from the flaw by pointing out something that's good – like turning up the radio and raving about the great sound system so you don't hear the engine knock.

Sometimes writers do exactly the same thing.

When this occurs, they're guilt of handwaving.

A term coined by Stewart Brand, handwaving is "distracting the reader with verbal fireworks to keep him from noticing a severe logic flaw." For example, the "Star Trek: The Original Series" episode "Miri" has our intrepid explorers discover an exact duplicate of our planet several hundred light years from this region of the galaxy. The device of a duplicate Earth allows a landing party to encounter a world on which only children live, as a life longevity project from 300 years before has gone bad, ensuring that once youth enter puberty they contract a fatal disease.

Unfortunately, exactly why there is a duplicate Earth several hundred light years from here is never addressed in the episode. It's an interesting concept but highly improbable. It piques viewers' interest – much in the same way that one waves their arms – and covers the issue of exactly why our crew would come across planet with humans on it. Once thought about, the unexplained flaws of a duplicate Earth to allow us to have a planet of humans to interact with merely undermines the episode's credibility.

To fix handwaving, you'll need to dump the plot device and instead address the logical flaw. That may require some major rethinking of the plot or character and possibly even a significant rewrite of sections of the story. In "Miri," that would mean not visiting a duplicate Earth. Instead, the humans on the planet might be descendants of a colonial expedition sent out three centuries before from Earth.

Such rewriting may take a lot of work, but the effort is worth it. After all, any reader eventually will hear that knocking engine in your story...

You Do It

Identify any severe logical flaws in your manuscript and revise the script accordingly. This may require more than one seven-minute a day session to accomplish.

Step 30. Use Plain English, Please

Ever read a sentence in a story and wonder why the author couldn't just use plain English?

The author is guilty of polysyllabism, or using a long word for effect even though a shorter word is better.

For example, the first sentence of this entry would have been written as: *Ever read a sentence in a story and excogitate why the author couldn't just use plain English?*

Excogitate, meaning to ponder seriously, is an example of polysyllabism.

Of course, the word "polysyllabism," meaning "a word with three or more syllables," is a play on the whole concept.

The problem with using too long of a word is that it's not in many readers' vocabularies. They'll miss the meaning of the sentence or will have to re-read the sentence to figure out what you meant.

In fact, using polysyllabism largely is the author showing off or handwaving ("See, I'm smart! I know big words!").

There is a time to use polysyllabism, though, and it's usually for humor. This often is done to great effect in science fiction, when characters such as genius scientists (like those B-grade movies), ultrasmart aliens (like Mr. Spock) or intelligent machines (like the android Data) use large words.

For the jokes to work, though, usually the reader must know what the character is referring to – so the words, while large, aren't necessarily obscure.

You Do It

Substitute words guilty of polysyllabism with regular words that most readers will understand (unless, of course, the long word is used for jocularity!).

Step 31. Pen Engaging Dialogue

No doubt your story will include dialogue in which characters speak to one another. Unfortunately, too many beginning writers drag their story into a furrow of tedium by poorly handling dialogue.

The problem is that their characters' dialogue too closely mirrors actual conversations.

Realistic dialogue in a story isn't a copy of how we really speak in everyday life. Our daily conversations are filled with niceties, formalities, repetition and the mundane. They often are tedious and even banal.

Writers can't afford to waste a word of their story on such dialogue. Instead, they should keep in mind that dialogue in a story – unlike real life – always must have a conversational goal. Dialogue is a means of characterization, a way for characters to push forward their agenda vital to the plot. Characters engage in competition and verbal combat via their dialogue.

Compare the following dialogue examples. This one attempts to mimic real life conversation:

"You know, Upir, I've changed. Wish I could help you."

The alien raised his hands. "But what of Ala and I? It took all three of us to lure the human spacecraft to that asteroid."

"But two of the humans died when the spacecraft crashed! I was the test subject for us; I volunteered so you would not die if it didn't work!"

"Well then, why did you leave us there?"

"It was the jump, it made me mad, you know. I did not know what I was doing!"

"You do now, right?"

"Yeah, I do. But I am powerless. You see, once human, you no longer can jump."

"Yeah, I know."

"You do? How?"

"The humans sent a rescue craft. Ala was near death, so he jumped."

"Oh, I see."

The following example, however, indicates the characters have goals to achieve. They use their conversation to further their personal agendas:

"I've changed, Upir. I can't help you."

"You know what will happen if you don't do as I say."

"I'm not cold anymore, Upir."

The alien raised his hand like a cat ready to strike. "Yes, Raphaelie, I can see that. You've got what you wanted. But what of Ala and I? It took all three of us to lure the human spacecraft to that asteroid. You will make amends for what you did."

"But two of the humans died when the spacecraft crashed! I was the test subject for us; I volunteered so you would not die if it didn't work!"

"Then why did you leave us there?"

"It was the jump, it made me mad. I did not know what I was doing!"

"But you do now."

"I am powerless. Once human, you can't jump."

"I know."

"How?"

"The humans sent a rescue craft. Ala was near death. He jumped."

"Why didn't you?"

"Because I wanted you."

Which one did you find was more interesting to read?

You Do It

Review your use of dialogue in your manuscript. Rewrite (and even delete) any dialogue in which characters do not further their personal agendas.

Step 32. Prevent Countersinking from Dragging Down Your Story

One way for an author to slow a story is to employ "countersinking." A term coined by science fiction writer Lewis Shiner, countersinking involves making explicit the very actions that the story implies. An example is: *"We need to hide," she said, asking him to seek cover.*

Countersinking is also known as "expositional redundancy" and for good reason; in the above example, the character's dialogue already directly states that she thinks they should hide. So why repeat it? Besides slowing the story's dramatic momentum, countersinking suggests the author lacks confidence in his or her storytelling ability.

The solution is simple: Cut the redundant wording to tighten your writing. The above ex-ample could be rewritten as: *"We need to hide," she said.*

You Do It

Delete all of the redundant wording in your story or chapter.

Step 33. Switch out Bookisms

Ever notice when reading a story that sometimes an odd word appears when "said" would do? For example, *"Well, I've never!" she blustered.*

If so, you've just come across a bookism. A term devised by science fiction writer James Patrick Kelly, a bookism is a long word that means "said."

Usually writers use a bookism to convey information that is not directly stated in dialogue or description. For example, in *"That could be the case," he admitted*, the fill-in for "said" – *admitted* – is intended to connote that the speaker acknowledges that there's some truth to a position or explanation that apparently the previous speaker gave.

Rather than tell readers how they should interpret a certain statement, writers almost are always better off to infer it. That may mean rewriting the dialogue or description.

In many cases, the writer already has inferred it. For example, in the previous paragraph's bookism, the speaker's statement implies that he acknowledges there's some truth to a position or explanation with which he disagrees. There's no need to emphasize it.

Another reason to not use bookisms is that really poor ones sometimes can result in an unintentional Tom Swifty, such as *"It's a unit of electric current," Tom amplified.*

Don't worry about overusing "said," a common reason authors like to use bookisms. "Said" is a nearly invisible word for most readers. In addition, during long exchanges of dialogue between two characters, attribution usually isn't needed for every line they speak, so many potential uses of "said" are deleted.

You Do It
Locate bookisms in your manuscript and replace them with "said."

Step 34. Silence the Laugh Track

Another way to tighten your writing is to leave out the laugh track. In comedy television shows, fake recorded laughter often is added to suggest that an audience is present – and to suggest to viewers at home that they also should find a joke humorous.

In your story, a laugh track is present when you also give readers hints about how they should react. American writer Lewis Shiner came up with the term.

Possible examples of a laugh track in your story might include characters laughing at their own jokes or crying when they feel emotional pain.

If you've written your story well enough, the reader shouldn't need to be told that the character is laughing or crying. The reader will feel the humor or inner turmoil themselves and can imagine the characters guffawing or weeping.

Indeed, a laugh track is telling rather than showing and so is a form of countersinking.

An exception (and there's always an exception!) is when characters have an emotional response that isn't "ordinary," such as laughing at an extremely inappropriate joke. This can help give readers a sense of what the character is really like – in this case uncouth and depending on the joke possibly racist, chauvinist or just plain strange.

You Do It

Look for spots in your manuscript where you've added a laugh track and delete them. If what you've written appears to need a word or phrase about the character expressing an emotion, then that line probably needs to be rewritten so readers can infer that.

Step 35. Crack a Joke – But Only for a Good Reason

Just as in real life when humor is used to ease tension in social situations or to bond with another person, so jokes and comedy serves a purpose in your story.

Unfortunately, a lot of novice writers don't quite know when to inject humor into their tales. The result is they either miss opportunities to use an effective narrative tool or they misuse (and quite often overuse) it.

There are a lot of good reasons to inject humor into your story. Among them:

■ **Plot device** – Comedy can help relieve tension. If a novel, short story or stage play has a number of gruesome murders in it, the reader can become numb to the tale's intensity. To that end, Shakespeare in "Macbeth" used a short humorous scene (the drunken porter scene) after Macbeth assassinates the king.

■ **Character development** – Jokes can be used to reveal information about characters, such as their foibles (via other characters making fun of them) or their values (as humor can suggest one's belief system.). These inferred facts about the characters then can be incorporated into the plot for good effect, such as Indiana Jones' fear of snakes in his various movies.

■ **Theme** – By making fun of an idea or of a character who represents a concept, humor can bring to light a story's message. There's nothing quite like a cutting quip to break a protagonist's knotty reasoning.

Unless you deliberately intend your story to be humorous – such as Douglas Adams' "A Hitch-hiker's Guide to the Galaxy" – be wary of overusing humor. Jokes and comedy that don't serve a purpose and that work more like asides to fill up space actually slow the story. In such situations, your characters or narrator are just clowning around.

You Do It

Review the humorous scenes in your manuscript. Do they serve a purpose? If they don't, delete them. In addition, are there spots in the story where humor might be added to relieve tension, build a character, or express the story's theme? If so, consider adding humor in those sections.

Step 36. Maintain the Reader's Illusion

As a novelist or short story writer, among your chief goals is to establish and maintain a fictional dream, which occurs when readers actually feel like they are experiencing what is being read. One way to achieve that is to establish consistency in your story.

Consistency involves providing details that maintain the readers' illusion of being in a different world. A number of writers use various terms to explain consistency; among them is Ursula K. LeGuin's "from Elfland to Poughkeepsie."

Consistency is more than making sure you don't write on one page that the sun rises in the north and then three pages later write it rises in the south. While that inconsistency certainly would need to be corrected, you'll want to think even deeper about your story.

For example, story details can contradict one another because facts established in one part wouldn't allow for facts presented later in the story to be true. In science fiction stories, this might occur when a civilization that's suffered a global nuclear war is still capable of spaceflight. The odds are against this occurring, because the infrastructure to support spaceflight (the manufacturing of space parts and ship fuel) and the launch facilities probably wouldn't exist if the war destroyed cities.

When writing your story, watch for these common consistency errors:

■ **Inadequate background** – Characters should have the experience to possess certain knowledge or to solve certain problems. For example, would someone who has never picked up a gun in his life know how to aim and fire it let alone hit the target?

■ **Excessive luck/coincidence** – The main character should be able to resolve the story's problem not because they got lucky but because of their skills, talents and grit.

■ **Insufficient background motivation** – For a character to be in a situation or to make a decision, they must have experienced something in their past that allows them to be involved. A teenage boy shouldn't know the correct strategy to win a war, for example – but he might if he were a history buff and his father had served as a military officer.

You Do It

Read your manuscript – or better yet have someone else read it – and look specifically for spots with inadequate background, excessive luck or coincidence, or insufficient background motivation. Rewrite the scenes to address those issues.

Color

Another set of stylistic techniques that gives your story a unique voice is color. This involves making your writing more vivid through descriptions, imagery and symbolism. During the pages ahead, we'll examine several methods you can use – and a few you should avoid – to pen a vibrant story.

Step 37. Add Color to Your Manuscript

Even if your story offers a lot of dramatic tension and the sentences are tightly constructed, it still can feel a bit monochrome or colorless. When that occurs, the writing probably is not particularly vivid.

Rather than read like a piece of fiction, the story instead will feel like a work of dry, emotionless journalism.

Consider this fairly colorless passage:

Kneeling before the car, Carl Steinar thought his wife appeared to be sleeping, but he knew that she'd simply lost too much blood. A tear fell from his eyes. In a single moment, every memory of their few short years with one another surfaced: the first night together; of how she loved Nebraska; of her hands as they caressed his neck; of their two boys. He stumbled back, tried to hold back the weeping.

The piece lacks several elements that could make it more vibrant:

■ **Descriptions** – To create a sense of the world where your story occurs, you'll want to describe the spatial setting, the time, and the characters. Not doing this is akin to watching a play without any scenery and with a sheet rather than costumes tossed over the characters. More on this in Step 39.

■ **Imagery** – Good fiction writing appeals to the readers' various senses – sight, smell, sound, taste and touch. Since people experience the world through their five senses, including them in a story helps the reader vicariously experience the fictional world. More on this in Step 41.

■ **Symbolism** – Descriptions and imagery can carry additional levels of meaning by being presented as similes, metaphors or other figurative language. Such connotations can carry great emotional weight. More on this in Step 42.

By using these techniques, the above passage could be rewritten as:

Kneeling before the car, all he could see was crimson blood. His wife appeared to be asleep, but he knew that crumpled body, jammed between the driver's seat and projecting steering wheel, had simply lost too much vital fluid for it to be true. Then a mist of lavender netting covered her, as if she was a bride about to wake, and Carl Steinar realized he was viewing Gwen through his tears. In a single moment, every memory of their few short years with one another surfaced: the first night together; of how she loved Nebraska's yellow sky and the wind's glorious cry, of her soothing hands as she caressed his neck; of their two little boys. He stumbled back, lay fetal position in the middle of the road, and shaking his head desperately tried to hold back the weeping.

This version of the passage is more vibrant because it actually describes the scene. For example, the reader can better visualize the car wreck through the description of his wife's body and of where Carl Steinar lays in the roadway. The passage also makes much better use of imagery. We have an array of colors in the scene, such as the crimson blood, Nebraska's yellow sky, the lavender netting that is Carl's tears. There also is an appeal to senses beyond sight, specifically touch through a description of the wife's smooth hands caressing his neck, and of sound via *the wind's glorious cry*. Finally, the passage even makes use of symbolism with the simile *as if she were a bride about to wake*, which emotes Carl's feelings toward her and his sense of loss.

You Do It

Identify passages in your manuscript that read monochromatic or like straight journalism. Mark them and begin to think of ways that you might add description, imagery and symbolism to give them more flavor.

Step 38. Make Use of Local Dexterity

One of the kindest things writers can do for their readers is employ "local dexterity." This occurs when images, sentences, paragraphs and scenes are pleasurable to read because of their vividness.

To achieve the descriptions, imagery and symbolism in your story must work in concert with all of the other techniques discussed so far in this book. Imagery that is written in passive voice, for example, will remain weak writing.

Consider this passage:

The stuffy house was dark from the drawn curtain. Yellowed Cape Cods were over the kitchen sink. Boxes and stacks of newspapers lined the walls. Abbie saw one pile with by an edition dating back some 15 years. The furniture was at least that old as well. Peter was unhappy for suggesting they go inside. Sitting at the dining table, he pushed away dirty dishes and an open cereal box. Lyle, his eyes caked with gray dust and belly sticking out even farther than usual, slumped in a chair across from him. Their father went into the living room, his mouth open. He was like a senile old man trying to gain his bearings.

The passage could use a little tightening, some variety in sentence structure, and definitely active voice verbs. It could be rewritten as:

The wind died as they entered the stuffy house, dark from the drawn curtain and yellowed Cape Cods over the kitchen sink. Boxes and stacks of newspapers lined the walls. Abbie noticed one pile topped by an edition dating back some 15 years. The furniture appeared at least that old as well, and for a moment Peter reproached himself for suggesting they go inside. Sitting at the dining table, he pushed away dirty dishes and an open cereal box, while Lyle, his eyes caked with gray dust and belly sticking out even farther than usual, slumped in a chair across from him. Their father lolled into the living room, however, his mouth hanging open as if a senile old man trying to gain his bearings.

Notice how the second passage describes the house and three men in a clear and striking manner compared to the way it originally was written. As both passages' images are life-like, readers can visualize the scene as they would an immediate experience – but since the second passage makes better use of diction and narrative drive, its imagery is more effective.

Be careful of using local dexterity to hide the absence of drama or conflict, however. If you enjoyed reading a passage you wrote but keep telling yourself that nothing happened in it, you're going overboard with local dexterity.

You Do It

Read the passages you marked in Step 37. Determine if their diction and narrative drive also need some work. Write notes next to the passages about how to improve the diction or narrative drive. We'll address those issues during the steps ahead.

Step 39. Ensure Descriptive Writing Serves a Purpose

When creating your story's setting or explaining what your characters are doing, you'll need to use description. Description is necessary to move along the plot and to create tone. You even can create resonance in your writing by layering the description with symbolic meaning – but more on that later.

When writing description, always make sure it serves a purpose. Any description should move along the plot, help develop characters, and heighten the dramatic tension. If it's solely being used to establish the location of the story or to indicate a background character's actions, keep the description quick and simple.

You can ensure your description serves a purpose by only using those details that capture the "essence" of a place/moment/character. For example, if a landscape is supposed to be forebodeing, then describe it as such by noting the lack of water, the difficult terrain, the strange outcroppings of rock. A foreboding environment would not be lush and comfortably warm.

As reporting this "essence," always use sensory details rather than internalized ones. Sensory details (*green, tart, quiet, rough*) are specific rather than general. Internalized details (*happy, melancholy, guilty, barbaric*) amount to editorializing and give no real impression of what is being described.

If you've assembled several details to help relay the essence of a place or a character, you might divide the descriptions into three sections. For example, start with the foreground, then in the next couple of sentences go the middle, and at the paragraph's end go to the background. Or try left-center-right or sky-eye level-ground.

Finally, always remain cautious about offering

lengthy descriptions. Such writing in novels obviously can be longer than those in short stories. Still, the lengthier the description, the greater the chance that the reader will forget what's going on in the story.

You Do It

Review the descriptive scenes in your manuscript. Do they serve a purpose by capturing the essence of a place, character or moment? If not, rewrite those lines or paragraphs. Also, are there places where you might add description that captures a place's, character's or moment's essence so that you might move along the plot, help develop characters and dramatic tension? If so, write some description for those parts of the story.

Step 40. Describe what's in Front of You, Not what's in the Rear-view Mirror

When writing action scenes, avoiding rear-view mirror descriptions typically is a good idea. In such a description, an object is described only after they've been part of the action. For example, *He slid into the cave hole that his foot had just felt.* This type of writing allows the reader to see the setting only after the character has interacted with it – in short, it's like looking at a landscape through a rear-view mirror.

Such writing diminishes the reader's ability to feel the story's dramatic tension and to sense the character's urgency. It strains the story's verisimilitude because the character appears to be extremely lucky as he is able to get out of any jam thanks to the author's good blessings.

This type of description is a common error of novice writers, so not surprisingly this term often is most heard is writing workshops. In fact, it was coined at the Cambridge Science Fiction Workshop.

To avoid rear-mirror descriptions, lay out in advance the setting, including all objects with which the characters later will interact. In addition, reverse the order of sentences or phrasing within them so that the object appears before it is acted upon. The above example of a rear-view mirror description could be rewritten as: *His foot slipped into an opening in the dark rock. It felt just large enough to accommodate him. "This must be the cave entrance," he thought. He slid into the hole.*

You Do It

Review your manuscript for rear-view mirror descriptions. If you find any, revise that section of the story so that the descriptions appear in the chronologically correct spot.

Step 41. Incorporate Imagery into Your Story

When creating your story's setting or explaining what your characters are doing, you'll need to use imagery. This is necessary to move along the plot and to establish tone.

When describing a landscape, character or action, you'll need to appeal to one or more of the senses that people use to perceive the world. There are five senses:

■ **Sight** – What we can see with our eyes, as in *Nevar examined the black hole ahead. It had the diameter of a mere asteroid. X-rays shot from the white-hot disc at its center, each ring farther out as darkening from white to blue.*

■ **Sound** – What we can hear; for example, *As Nevar quietly assisted, her brother tapped here and there.*

■ **Smell** – The scent of something, as in *The smell of sweat trickling down her temple overtook the faint whiff of ozone permeating the cockpit.*

■ **Touch** – What we can feel when things come into contact with our bodies (or they can be a description of the body's sensation of touch), as in *Nevar's back ached.*

■ **Taste** – The flavor of something when it comes into contact with the tongue, as in *Her mouth grew dry.*

Often flat stories fail to appeal to more than just one or two senses.

Yet using as many of the senses as possible makes a scene more real. In everyday life, we experience all of these five senses at all times. Sitting in a coffee shop writing this entry, I see the barista racing to and fro as filling an order, hear the hushed voices of the couple sitting behind me as they try to keep their disagreement from bursting into a public scene, taste the bitter coffee, catch a whiff of the pear-scented perfume of a woman passing my table on her way to the counter, shiver at the cold breeze from the air conditioner that is working on overdrive. In fiction, the key is to make these different senses work with one another to create tone.

When writing imagery, follow these guidelines:

■ **Make sure it serves a purpose** – Any description should move along the plot and help develop characters and dramatic tension. If it's solely being used to establish the location of the story or to indicate a background character's actions, keep the description quick and simple.

■ **Avoid flowery prose simply for the sake of waxing poetic** – Purple prose only makes the story campy. See Step 47.

■ **Remain cautious about offering lengthy descriptions** – Descriptions in novels obviously can be longer than those in short stories. Still, the longer the description, the greater the chance that it will cause the reader to forget what's going on in the story.

■ **Capture the "essence" of a place/moment /character through description** – If a landscape is supposed to be inviting, then describe it as such by noting the ferns hanging over the waterfall, the bubbling brook, and the shade from a green willow. An inviting environment would not be excessively hot with the sun beating down.

■ **Use sensory details rather than internalized ones** – Sensory details (*blue, sour, loud, smooth*) are specific rather than general. Internalized details (*angry, pleased, innocent, civilized*) amount to using fuzzy words and give no real impression of what is being described.

You Do It

Review your manuscript for places where you might add imagery that appeals to the senses. Try to get at least four of the five senses in your story (That should be easy enough – you probably already appeal to the sense of sight, so there's just three senses to go!).

Step 42. Layer Imagery with Symbolic Meaning

Descriptions and imagery can carry additional levels of meaning by being presented as figurative language. Such wording compares two items, usually by giving one symbolic meaning.

For example, in *Abbie's presence lingered in his mind like dew atop grass on a pleasant morning*, the character's thoughts about the woman are compared to dew atop grass on a pleasant morning, inferring that he finds her lovely. The image of *dew atop grass on a pleasant morning* is symbolic. The reader knows that the character is enamored by her; using this technique is much more vibrant than simply writing, *He found himself enamored with Abbie.*

There are many kinds of figurative language, but three reign over all others, if only because they are more commonly used:

■ **Simile** – This occurs when two objects are compared by using the word "like" or "as": *His forehead was heavily creased, like an overfolded map* (The forehead creases are compared to that of an overfolded map.).

■ **Metaphor** – Slightly more sophisticated than a simile, a metaphor makes a comparison without using "like" or "as": *Lyle drooped as Peter interrupted him again. Just like my brother, Lyle thought, always slamming a door in my face* (Being made to feel unimportant is compared to having a door slammed in one's face).

■ **Personification** – This technique gives human traits to a nonhuman object or a concept: *The flowers danced in the wind* (The flowers' movement is compared to dancing, a human activity).

Such connotations can carry great emotional weight. That's because through figurative language a writer either infers an emotion by giving it concreteness via the comparison or by presenting an evocative image that goes beyond the word's literal meaning. Typically, unlike things are compared, which if it's an apt comparison, bolsters the image's vibrancy.

You Do It

Are there spots in your manuscript where figurative language might be used? Try to add one simile, one metaphor, and one use of personification to your text.

Step 43. Hide an Easter Egg

Sometimes the real pleasure of writing – and reading – isn't entirely about the well-crafted tale with a fast-moving plot involving intriguing characters set in a well-described landscape. After all, penning such a story entails a lot of sweat, and readers expect nothing less than a well-developed piece.

Instead, the real smile comes when the author leaves a special treat for the reader, such as hiding some surprise not germane to the story. These surprises are called "Easter eggs," a term science fiction writing workshops have borrowed from the jargon of computer programming.

For example, an author might encode with the first letters of consecutive sentences some message to the reader. In other instances, the author may use obscure allusions. In my novel "Windmill," for example, the name of one of the main characters is Peter, a young man who has turned emotionless to deal with the childhood loss of his mother. The meaning of the name Peter is "rock" or "stone" – appropriate for a man who has "hardened" himself over the years. No reader needs to know the meaning of Peter's name to understand the story, but those who do pick up a little something extra.

The pleasure for the author is akin to being part of an "inside joke." The pleasure for the reader comes in possessing a deeper understanding of the piece – or at least in knowing that he's one of the few who got the "in-joke"! It strengthens the bond between writer and reader.

You Do It

Think back to a spot in your story where you might add an obscure reference that won't slow the story's flow but that a careful reader will recognize as a nod to someone or an idea.

Step 44. Coax Readers to Eat Story's Veggies by Promising Cookies

If you want to impress readers, give them a cookie. A term coined by CSFW's David Smith, a cookie is some item in the text that rewards readers paying close attention to the story.

A cookie might be a clever turn of phrase, a powerful descriptive image, or an allusion. While the cookie may not be necessary to the telling of the story (just as a cookie isn't necessary to a meal), it does add to the tale by enriching it (sort of like desert after you've eaten your veggies).

This is unlike card tricks in the dark, in which writers show off their talent in a way that slows the story – such as a humorous scene that's included solely for the sake of the writer demonstrating that he or she can write a humorous scene.

Cookies also are a little different than an Easter egg, which usually is a hidden reference to something, such as using a word from another language that means "villain" for the name of a hostile alien race in a science fiction story. If readers don't catch the reference, it won't hurt the story, and hiding the Easter egg is done is such a way that it doesn't slow the story. Cookies are much more obvious.

Why add cookies to the story? Because they encourage readers to pay even more attention to the tale – just as cookies for dessert encourage kids to eat all their peas and carrots during the main course.

Such readers, hopefully, will grow to appreciate the writer's abilities and then pick up more of his or her books.

In fact, other writers' cookies probably are the reason you came to like reading them and books in general. Lazy and less able readers tend to miss cookies and so don't get why so many people like a specific writer or book.

You Do It

Identify a spot where you might add a cookie to your manuscript. Ideally, you'd want one every couple of pages.

Step 45. Include Clever In-Jokes by Tuckerizing

One way of rewarding the careful reader is by tuckerizing. This involves naming secondary characters or offstage icons after people or objects many readers would recognize as a sort of in-joke.

For example, in Larry Niven's and David Gerrold's novel "The Flying Sorcerers," all of the gods are name after famous science fiction personalities, such as H.G. Wells and Gene Roddenberry (creator of "Star Trek"). Sometimes "Star Trek" novels use series staff names for characters.

The term is named after Wilson Tucker, a prominent science fiction critic and fan perhaps best known for coming up with the term "space opera." He often used names of his friends in his science fiction stories, the source of the term "tuckerizing."

Successful tuckerizing requires being unobtrusive. The name never should stand in the way of the story and its dramatic tension. To that end, Niven and Gerrold altered the spelling of their gods so that H. G. Wells was "Ouells" and Roddenberry was "Rotn'bair."

You Do It

Does an opportunity present itself to tuckerize in your story? If it does, take advantage of it! Don't force the issue, though – remember, good tuckerizing, like an Easter egg, doesn't draw attention to itself.

Step 46. Stay Inbounds when Writing Descriptively

Sometimes in our efforts to succeed, we overdo it. While training for a marathon, we run too many miles at first rather than build our strength, or while baking a cake we add too much of one ingredient in hopes of spicing it up. The results usually are disastrous and require that we start over.

So it is with descriptive writing as well. As striving to deliver vivid, engaging writing, we actually can make our writing sound worse.

There are a number of ways that writers can overdo it. The most common errors among novices are:

■ **Fat writing** – This involves using extraneous and showy verbiage. Writing instructors often refer to it as "purple prose." For example, *Galen's mysterious, stygian eyes gawped in utter awe at Samantha's pure, angelic being.* More on this in Step 47.

■ **Foreground to** – Writers shouldn't draw attention to some object in their story purely for artistic effect. This might mean you've written a poetic-sounding but meaningless image, such as *gelatinous sneer*. Doing so actually slows the story by decreasing the dramatic tension. More on this in Step 48.

■ **Pushbutton words** – Rather than describe one's physical responses, the writer resorts to overused words intended to invoke an emotion, like *dance* as in *And so the slow dance of their love began*. Typically they don't invoke any response other than a yawn. More on this in Step 49.

Just as you want to know how to improve your descriptive writing by recognizing techniques that can make your story more vibrant, so you also want to be aware of when you've gone too far. It's like a football or a basketball player being aware of the out-of-bounds line.

You Do It

With a colored pencil, pen or highlighter, mark the descriptive passages in your manuscript. We'll return to what you've marked and decide if the lines should be deleted or rewritten.

Step 47. Work off the Fat from Overwritten Descriptions

Fabio's robust, bulging arms swathed them-selves in a bronze casing about Shannon's flawless, wilting body. Her velvety, wine-colored lips arched toward his as her sparkling sapphire eyes gazed into his brilliant, glowing emerald pupils and she in turn sheathed his body with her elongated, grace-ful, snow white arms. They were one at last.

Wasn't that pretty? Maybe, if you like pigs with lipstick. It's a good example of fat writing.

Fat writing, a term coined by CSFW's Sarah Smith, is "unnecessary and grandiose verbiage." You may have heard writing instructors refer to it as "verdant greenery" or "purple prose."

You want to trim the fat off your writing. If you stuff it with grandiosities, you're just showing off, or demonstrating your writing skills not to advance the story but merely to prove you've got a way with words.

Okay, so maybe you're good at creating a clever image with consonance and alliteration, but what is the point of that image if it doesn't advance the story? It's just fat on your piece...and while your story can be lean, muscled or curvy, you don't want flab hanging from it.

Fixing it is easy: Simplify your sentences and say exactly what you mean. For example, the first paragraph could be rewritten as: *Fabio and Shannon embraced and gazed into one another's eyes. They were one at last.* Notice how all of the extra adverbs and adjective were deleted.

Giving your writing a good liposuction doesn't mean it can't be evocative or sensuous. Quite the contrary. It will be more so after you've toned and shaped your sentences.

You Do It

Look back at the descriptive writing you highlighted in Step 46. Cut away extra adjectives and adverbs from overwritten descriptions.

Step 48. Shun Beautiful Writing Done for Beauty's Sake

Ever read a beautiful image in a story but then ask yourself, "So what?"

If so, you've probably been a victim of the foreground to trick. A term created by CSFW's Sarah Smith, "foreground to" occurs when you draw attention to some object in your story purely for artistic effect.

A type of card tricks in the dark, it's just another way of showing off. Consider this example:

He stood 5-foot-11 and had a vicious mustache.

Sure, it's descriptive – and *vicious mustache* sounds cool with its use of alliteration and assonance – but it doesn't move the story forward. First, *5-foot-11* is an average height, so there's nothing remarkable about it and probably would only need to appear if the author wanted to show that the person was average; but *vicious mustache* instead suggests an atypical character. By giving the height, the author merely appears to want to demonstrate to the reader that he's done his due diligence and thought about what the character looks like. Secondly, the purpose of *vicious mustache* appears to be simply to show that the author is capable of creating a poetic-sounding image. After all, exactly what is a *vicious mustache*?

To be effective, an image or description – like every other word in the story – should serve a purpose. For example, it might be used to develop a character by offering descriptions that manifest personality traits. Or it might be used to set atmosphere and mood. Or it might be used for thematic purposes, such as drawing parallels between two objects so as to show how a situation is analogous.

But to do it solely to demonstrate you're capable of writing a pretty simile or description isn't a great idea.

You Do It

Review the descriptive writing you highlighted in Step 46, looking for superfluous descriptions. Delete them – or better yet, rewrite them so that they do serve a purpose.

Step 49. Avoid Using Weak Pushbutton Words

Sometimes rather that finding a truly evocative term, writers get lazy and use pushbutton words. Pushbutton words attempt to evoke an emotional response from readers without appealing to their critical faculties or intellect. American writer Lewis Shiner coined the term.

Examples of pushbutton words include: *dreams, poet, song* and *tears* in sentences like these:

■ *He wondered if his dreams would ever come true.*

■ *Her heart sang like a poet's.*

■ *He could not shake the image of her smile, which remained in his head like a pretty song.*

■ *Tears welled in her eyes.*

Each of these words is intended to evoke an emotional response (dreams=hope, poet's=love, song=beauty, tears=sadness), as if the writer says, "I want readers to feel sadness, so I will push the button marked 'tears' and that's what they'll feel." Because writers overuse these words, however, the stimuli doesn't work so well; there is a bad connection between the button and the reader's response. If using a pushbutton word in your writing, delete the sentence and start over. Seek another way to be evocative.

You Do It

Looking back at the descriptive writing you highlighted in Step 46, replace the wording with more redolent writing.

Step 50. Deliver an Eyeball Kick to Readers

One of the best ways to keep readers engaged

in a story is to give them an eyeball kick. A term coined by science fiction writer Rudy Rucker, an eyeball kick is "a perfect, telling detail that creates an instant and powerful visual image," according to the Science Fiction Writers of America.

Consider this example an of eyeball kick (in bold) from the novel "Quantum: Event Horizon" by Zac McNabb, in which the foster parent Ron speaks of his two children:

"It's alright. The Lord has blessed her with good judgment. I believe the Lord has blessed Samuel with the wisdom needed to keep family secrets. Luke 8:10 says 'The knowledge of the secrets of the kingdom of God has been given to you. But to others I speak in parables, so that, though seeing, they may not see; though hearing, they may not understand.'" **Ron picks the raw meat out of his teeth.** *"That means God wants you to honor your families, and it's ok to keep secrets, because others may not understand."*

What makes an instant and powerful image? First, it must be evocative, meaning it brings out strong emotions or feelings in readers. *Ron picks the raw meat out of his teeth* accomplishes this by rousing a sense of revulsion in the reader. In addition, the image adds to the story's meaning by providing a new layer of understanding or an insight into it. The reader suddenly knows that Ron is a child abuser of some sort. In this way, the image creates instant understanding.

Be careful of overdoing it, though. An image that tries too hard to be evocative can misfire, undercutting the story. Delivering an eyeball kick requires a precise aim.

You Do It

Read through the descriptions in your manuscript. You probably have some eyeball kicks in there. If not, try to add one or two to the story.

Index

ABOUT THE AUTHOR

Rob Bignell is the owner and chief editor of Inventing Reality Editing Service, which meets the editing and proofreading needs of writers both new and published. Several of his short stories in the literary and science fiction genres have been published, and he is the author of the literary novel "Windmill," the nonfiction "Best Sights to See," "Hikes with Tykes," "Headin' to the Cabin," and "Hittin' the Trail" hiking guidebooks, and the poetry collection "Love Letters to Sophie's Mom." For more than two decades, he worked as an award-winning journalist, with half of those years spent as an editor. He spent another seven years as an English teacher or a community college journalism instructor. He holds a Master's degree in English and a Bachelor's in journalism and English.

CHECK OUT
THE OTHER BOOKS
IN THIS SERIES

➤ **7 Minutes a Day to Your Bestseller** – Novel writers receive expert advice on topics like motivating yourself to write, starting your story with exciting opening lines, creating intriguing characters, mastering the craft of writing to elevate your style, and pitching your story to potential publishers.

➤ **7 Minutes a Day to a Self-Published Book** – Whether writing a novel or nonfiction, whether planning to print a paperback or an ebook, this book guides you through the self-publishing process, from the title page to the index, from designing a cover to formatting your text.

➤ **7 Minutes a Day to Promoting Your Book** – You'll develop a strategy that will get articles about your self-published book in newspapers, magazines, on radio and television programs, posted on blogs and linked to on websites, while landing you book signings and readings, all at virtually no cost.

ORDER ONLINE
inventingrealityediting.wordpress.com/
home/my-books

WANT TO BECOME
A BETTER WRITER?

Follow this book's blog,
where you'll find:

☞ **Advice for making your**
writing stronger

☞ **Great tips**
about self-publishing

☞ **Questions about writing**
and marketing answered

☞ **Product reviews**

☞ **News about the book series**
and author

VISIT ONLINE
inventingrealityeditingservice.typepad.
com/inventing_reality_editing

NEED
AN EDITOR?

Having your book, business document or academic paper proofread or edited before submitting it can prove invaluable. In an economic climate where you face heavy competition, your writing needs a second eye to give you the edge. The author of the "7 Minutes a Day..." writing guidebook series can provide that second eye.

FIND OUT MORE AT:

inventingrealityediting. wordpress.com/home

Made in the USA
Columbia, SC
22 December 2018